Great Artists

Edgar Degas

By Craig Boutland

Gareth Stevens
PUBLISHING

Please visit our website, www.garethstevens.com. For a free color catalog of all our high-quality books, call toll free 1-800-542-2595 or fax 1-877-542-2596.

Cataloging-in-Publication Data

Names: Boutland, Craig.
Title: Edgar Degas / Craig Boutland.
Description: New York : Gareth Stevens, 2023. | Series: Great artists |
Includes glossary and index.
Identifiers: ISBN 9781538277010 (pbk.) | ISBN 9781538277034 (library bound) |
ISBN 9781538277027 (6 pack) | ISBN 9781538277041 (ebook)
Subjects: LCSH: Degas, Edgar, 1834-1917--Juvenile literature. | Painters--France--
Biography--Juvenile literature.
Classification: LCC ND553.D3 B658 2023 | DDC 759.4--dc23

Published in 2023 by
Gareth Stevens Publishing
29 E. 21st Street
New York, NY 10010

For Brown Bear Books Ltd:
Design Manager: Keith Davis
Designer: John Woolford
Picture Manager: Sophie Mortimer
Children's Publisher: Anne O'Daly

Picture Credits
Cover: Bridgeman Images.
Alamy: Asar Studios 27; Bridgeman Images: 12–13, 14–15, 20–21, 24–25, Christie's Images 7, CSG CIC Glasgow Museums Collection 18–19, Museum of Fine Arts, Boston/S.A. Denio Collection 16–17, Luisa Ricciarini 22–23, Stapleton Collection 8–9, Robert A. Waller Fund 26; Museum of Fine Arts, Boston: 10; Public Domain: Harvard Art Museum 8, National Gallery of Art, Washington, D.C. 9; Shutterstock: Alessio Catelli 5, Everett Collection 4, 6, Ivor Golovniov 11, Konstantin Kuznetcov 3.
Special Thanks to Bridgeman Images.

Printed in the United States of America

CPSIA compliance information: Batch #CSGS23: For further information contact Gareth Stevens, New York, New York at 1-800-542-2595.
Find us on

Contents

Life Story

Edgar Degas was a master at painting dancers and horses. He was part of the group known as the Impressionists. Sadly, he went nearly blind when he was older.

Edgar Degas was born in Paris, France, in 1834. His family was wealthy. His grandfather had started a bank, and Edgar's father ran the bank in France. His mother was from a French family that had settled in America. Edgar's mother died when the young boy was just 13 years old.

Edgar's father loved art. He encouraged his son to work hard at drawing and painting. However, Edgar's father thought that art would be a hard way to make money. He wanted his son to be a lawyer.

Birth name: **Hilaire-Germain-Edgar de Gas (he shortened his name to Degas)**

Born: **July 19, 1834, Paris, France**

Died: **September 27, 1917, Paris, France**

Nationality: **French**

Field: **Painting and sculpture**

Movement: **Realism and Impressionism**

Influenced by: **Jean-Auguste-Dominique Ingres, Gustave Courbet, Édouard Manet**

Self-Portrait
Edgar Degas, 1855–56

Monmartre

Edgar set up his studio in Montmartre. This part of Paris is still popular with artists today.

A love of painting

Edgar started to study law, but his real love was painting. At age 20, he began taking painting lessons with an artist called Louis Lamothe. Edgar spent hours in the Louvre Museum in Paris copying the pictures by great painters. Unlike many young artists, he had no money worries.

At the age of 22, Edgar went to Italy to study artists such as Leonardo da Vinci. He stayed with an aunt in Florence and visited galleries there and in Rome. Edgar came back to Paris in 1859. He set up a studio in a part of the city called Montmartre.

Famous Paintings:

Young Spartans Exercising 1860
Racehorses at Longchamp 1874
The Dance Class 1875–76
The Absinthe Drinkers 1876
Woman in a Tub 1885

Art is not what you see but what you make others see.

Family portrait

While he was in Italy, Edgar worked on a portrait of his aunt and her family. He continued to paint portraits in France. Edgar also painted scenes from history and stories from the Bible. He showed some of his paintings at the Salon. This was the biggest art show in Paris. It was a place for young artists to get noticed.

In 1862, Edgar met a painter called Édouard Manet. They became friends. Both artists came from wealthy families. They shared an interest in horse racing, music, and the theater.

The Salon

The Salon in Paris was the most important art exhibition in France. Each year, a jury chose paintings to include in an annual exhbitition. The people who chose the paintings had traditional views about art. They liked a realistic style and great scenes from history. It was hard for a young artist with new ideas to get selected.

Impressionists

Édouard introduced Edgar to a group of artists who wanted to paint in a new way. They often painted outside, using quick brushstrokes to capture a moment in time. The group became known as Impressionists.

Poppy Fields near Argenteuil, by Claude Monet, 1875

Édouard Manet only painted two self-portaits.

Self-Portait with Palette
Édouard Manet, 1875

Going to war

In 1870, France went to war with Prussia (a part of Germany). Edgar joined the army. At shooting practice, he found out that he had bad eyesight. It was the first sign of the eye problems that would trouble him later in life.

After the war, Edgar visited his mother's family in the United States. New Orleans, Louisiana, where they lived, was the center of the cotton trade. Edgar loved the city's white buildings and the steamboats on the river. He painted portraits of his American relatives and pictures of life in the city.

Important People

Auguste de Gas – Edgar's father, who encouraged his interest in art

Louis Lamothe – teacher

Édouard Manet – fellow painter who introduced him to Impressionism

Mary Cassatt – American artist who became a good friend

Photography

Photography started to become popular around the same time as the Impressionists. Degas was fascinated by photography and owned several cameras. He took photos of his friends and used photographs as reference for some of his paintings. Some of his paintings even cut off people at the edge of the picture, just as photograph snapshots do.

Return to Paris

Edgar came back to Paris in 1873. In 1874, his father died, and Edgar found out that his brother owed lots of money. Edgar paid off the debts. For the first time in his life, he had to sell his paintings. Around this time, the Impressionist artists decided to break away from the Salon. They wanted to put on their own shows.

Key Places

Paris – France
Rome – Italy
New Orleans – United States

They put on their first exhibition in 1874. The show wasn't a success. Critics didn't understand what the artists were trying to do. They thought the paintings looked sloppy and unfinished. Edgar, however, did well. He painted new subjects, but he had the skills of the old classical artists.

Edgar probably took this photograph of himself in 1865. He enjoyed experimenting with new technology.

Later years

By the age of 50, Edgar was earning good money from his art. He was so successful that he didn't need to take part in exhibitions anymore. Art dealers came straight to him to buy his paintings. But he was starting to go blind and finding it harder to work. He began working with pastels rather than oil paint. This helped him get closer to the surface of his pictures. He worked more in sculpture, where he could use his sense of touch.

Edgar never married but had lots of friends. However, as he grew older he became lonelier. He fell out with a lot of his friends and went almost completely blind. Because of his eyesight, he produced no work in the last few years of his life. He died, aged 83, in 1917.

Edgar's sculpture of a 14-year-old dancer is very lifelike. It has real clothes on a bronze model.

How Degas Painted

Edgar was famous as one of the first Impressionists. But he didn't like that name. He thought of himself as a "realist," someone who painted life as it really is. But he was closer to the Impressionists than to any other painters.

Unlike the Impressionists, Edgar did not enjoy painting outdoors. He preferred to work in his studio. He was more interested in painting people than landscapes. Edgar thought about the composition of a picture before he started to paint it. He made lots of sketches first. Then he arranged the objects just as he wanted them. The Impressionists wanted to show things as they really are. Edgar wanted to do this, too. He painted people doing everyday activities, such as washing clothes and ironing.

Japanese art started to appear in France in the 1850s.

Pastels

As he grew older, Edgar used color more freely. As his eyesight got worse, he often used pastels instead of oil paints. He sometimes applied fine steam to the pastels to make the colors gleam.

Blue Dancers
Edgar Degas, c. 1897

Old ways and new ideas

Edgar trained in a traditional way. He learned how to draw and he copied the paintings of great classical painters. But he had a passion for learning new techniques and styles. He experimented with different media, including oil paints, pastels, printmaking, and sculpture. He was inspired by Japanese prints. They often showed subjects from unusual angles. Edgar tried this, too. He also tried out photography, which was new at the time. He sometimes cut off a figure at the edge of the picture, just like a photograph.

Impressionist painters

Claude Monet

Édouard Manet

Pierre-Auguste Renoir

Camille Pissarro

Alfred Sisley

Mary Cassatt

The Bellelli Family

Edgar started this picture when he was staying in Italy. He painted it between 1858 and 1867.

In 1858, Edgar stayed with his Aunt Laura in Florence. He studied the paintings in the famous Uffizi Gallery there. While he was staying with his aunt, he decided to paint a portrait of her family. The painting shows Laura, her husband Baron Gennaro, and their two daughters. Edgar made sketches while he was in Italy. He painted the picture when he came back to France.

In the Frame

● The original painting *The Bellelli Family* is 79 inches (200 cm) tall and 99 inches (253 cm) wide.

● It was his biggest picture at that time. The figures are almost life-size.

● Edgar never sold this picture. He kept it in his studio until just before he died.

The two girls are Giula, aged 10, and Giovanna, aged 7. Giula is the more serious of the girls. Giovanna has tucked one leg under her skirt.

Laura is wearing a black dress because her father had recently died. His portrait is on the wall behind her.

Baron Gennaro has his back to the viewer. Edgar did not like his aunt's husband. Laura and Gennaro were unhappy together.

The family's pet dog is at the edge of the picture, behind Gennaro's chair.

DEGAS'S

Palette of the picture

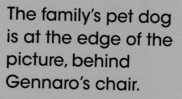

In 1872, Edgar decided to visit his mother's relatives in New Orleans. He stayed with his uncle and brothers.

Cotton was an important crop in the United States. Edgar's family in New Orleans bought and sold cotton. His uncle ran the business. Edgar's brothers, René and Achille, worked with their uncle. Edgar painted this picture of their busy office in 1873.

In the Frame

The original painting *The Cotton Exchange, New Orleans* is 29 inches (74 cm) tall and 36 inches (92 cm) wide.

Degas finished this painting in America and had it shipped to France.

He hoped to sell this painting to a cotton importer in Manchester, England, but the deal fell through.

Edgar's uncle, Michel, is at the front of the picture. He is inspecting a sample of cotton.

Edgar painted the cotton on the table with light, bright colors.

Edgar's brother René is in the middle of the picture. He is reading a newspaper.

DEGAS'S

Palette of the picture

Everybody has talent at 25. The difficult thing is to have it at 50.

Racehorses at Longchamp

Edgar loved painting horses and he enjoyed going to the races. He painted this picture in 1874.

Horse racing was a fairly new sport in France. Longchamp Racecourse, on the edge of Paris, had been built in 1857. It was a fashionable place for wealthy French people to go, including Edgar and his friend Édouard Manet. The painting shows racehorses and their jockeys after a race. Edgar rarely painted a race in action. He preferred to show what went on behind the scenes.

In the Frame

- The original painting *Racehorses at Longchamp* is 12 inches (30 cm) tall and 16 inches (40 cm) wide.

- Edgar made more than 90 paintings and drawings of racehorses during his career.

- Many of Edgar's racehorse paintings are done in pastels, but *Racehorses at Longchamp* is an oil painting.

- Edgar's friend, Édouard Manet, also painted pictures of the racecourse at Longchamp.

The horse at the left is pulling away from the others. Edgar was fascinated by the way horses move.

The jockeys' shirts are called silks. Their bright colors stand out against the browns of the horses and the green grass.

DEGAS'S

Palette of the picture

The horse in the center is standing still. It is turning its head to look at the other horses.

The Rehearsal

Edgar loved to paint the ballet. This is one of his first paintings of dancers. He painted it between 1874 and 1877.

Edgar was known as a painter of dancers. He watched them in rehearsals as well as in performances on stage. Edgar invited dancers to his studio. He drew them performing pirouettes and other difficult steps. In *The Rehearsal*, young ballerinas practice their steps. Their teacher, in the red shirt, looks on. Edgar wanted to show the hard work behind the elegant performances on stage.

In the Frame

● The original painting *The Rehearsal* is 23 inches (59 cm) tall and 33 inches (84 cm) wide.

● The aging dance master was based on a portrait of a famous dancer, Jules Perot.

● The dancer's mother in the black bonnet was modeled on Edgar's housekeeper, Sabine Neyt.

Degas painted a spiral staircase at the left of the picture. It cuts off some of the dancers so we can just see their legs.

A young girl sits with her back to the dancers. She is wrapped up against the cold. Her green shawl is in contrast with the red of the teacher's shirt.

Degas used pastel crayons to show details in the dancer's skirt.

DEGAS'S

Palette of the picture

The brushstrokes on the floor show soft shadows next to the sunlight that pours through the studio's window.

Miss La La at the Cirque Fernando

The painting shows an acrobat, Miss La La, performing in a circus. Degas painted this vivid scene in 1879.

The Cirque Fernando was built in 1875, near where Edgar lived. It soon became a popular attraction. Miss La La was one of the star acts. She was famous for her feats of incredible strength. In one of these, she held a rope between her teeth. She was pulled 70 feet (21 m) to the roof of the theater.

Miss La La is at the top and side of the painting. Most of the picture shows the theater's decorated ceiling.

In the Frame

- The original painting *Miss La La at the Cirque Fernando* is 46 inches (117 cm) tall and 30 inches (76 cm) wide.

- Edgar made a lot of drawings and sketches of Miss La La before he painted the picture.

- The painting was part of the Fourth Impressionist Exhibition in Paris.

Art is really a battle.

Edgar painted the picture looking up at Miss La La. It shows how the audience would have seen the act.

Strong steel girders support the ceiling.

The top of the column is painted with gold paint.

DEGAS'S

Palette of the picture

Women Ironing

Edgar painted this picture in 1884. It shows two women hard at work in a laundry.

Laundry was a big business in Paris at the time. The women employed in a laundry worked long hours. They were poorly paid. They worked in damp, cramped conditions and often caught illnesses such as bronchitis and tuberculosis. In this painting, the woman on the right is pressing the heavy iron with both hands. The other woman is stretching and yawning. She looks exhausted. Edgar wanted the painting to be realistic. He wanted to show how hard the women worked.

In the Frame

The original painting *Women Ironing* is 30 inches (76 cm) tall and 32 inches (82 cm) wide.

Laundresses (women who worked in a laundry) were one of Edgar's favorite subjects. He painted 27 paintings of laundresses between 1873 and 1895.

This painting is the third of the four versions that Edgar painted.

The upward movement of the yawning woman contrasts with the other woman's body bending over her iron.

Patches of canvas show through the paint, adding to the gritty feeling of the painting's subject.

The black iron stove heats the room and keeps the irons hot.

DEGAS'S

Palette of the picture

The woman's strong arms show that her work is hard and physical.

Combing the Hair

Edgar painted this picture in 1896. Although he was famous for painting dancers, he also liked to show scenes from everyday life.

The painting shows a girl having her hair combed by a maid or servant. The main colors are warm reds and oranges. The girl is leaning back in her chair. She has one hand on her head to stop her hair from being pulled. The comb is halfway through her hair. Both women have their eyes closed. Edgar painted a number of pictures of women combing their hair or having their hair combed.

In the Frame

- The original painting *Combing the Hair* is 45 inches (114 cm) tall and 58 inches (147 cm) wide.

- It stayed in Edgar's studio until he died.

- After Edgar's death, the painting was bought by another famous French artist, Henri Matisse.

Edgar used quick, loose brushstrokes for the young woman's face and hand.

Edgar uses dark lines to outline the hands, arms, and faces.

The yellow hairbrush is right at the edge of the table. Other objects on the table look unfinished, as if Edgar planned to go back to them later.

DEGAS'S

Palette of the picture

The lighter colors of the maid's blouse stand out against the bold red background.

What Came Next?

Edgar had a long career that lasted more than 50 years. He had strong opinions about art and he liked talking about them. Although he did not have any students, he influenced many younger artists.

One of these artists was Mary Cassatt. She was an American painter who moved to Paris. She met Edgar in 1877. They admired each other's work. Edgar had seen one of Mary's paintings at the Salon. He persuaded her to show her future work with the Impressionists. Mary learned a great deal from Edgar. She often joined him in his studio. Like him, she painted pictures with odd angles and unusual compositions. Mary introduced Edgar's work to art buyers in the United States. They were friends for nearly 40 years.

Mary Cassatt
is best known for her many paintings of mothers and their children.

The Bath
Mary Cassatt, 1910

Jean-Louis Forain
created many paintings of ballet dancers, just as Degas did.

Danseuses Dans les Coulisses
(Dancers in the Wings)
Jean-Louis Forain, 1905

Jean-Louis Forain

Edgar also encouraged a young French artist named Jean-Louis Forain. Jean-Louis was known for his sharp humor and sense of fun. He was very poor. He earned a small amount of money by selling cartoons to newspapers. Edgar introduced Jean-Louis to the theater and ballet. He encouraged Jean-Louis to show his paintings at the Impressionist exhibitions. The men became close friends, and Jean-Louis went to Edgar's funeral in 1917.

Important paintings by Mary Cassatt

Little Girl in a Blue Armchair 1878
Children Playing on the Beach 1884
Young Mother Sewing 1900
Mother and Child Reading 1913

How to Paint Like Degas

It's hard to paint like Degas. He spent years training and working. But you can have fun painting a ballet dancer, one of his favorite subjects.

WHAT YOU'LL NEED:

- Pencil
- Black marker
- Thick paintbrushes
- Paper
- Blue and orange watercolor paints

1.

Start by drawing a very loose outline of a dancer in pencil. Don't worry about detail. Just work on the shape.

2.

Mix blue paint with water and put it on a thick brush. Paint a thin layer of paint onto the dancer's skirt. It doesn't matter if you go outside the lines.

3.

Now, add blue to the top part of the dancer's dress. Then suggest a bow in her hair with a blob of blue.

4.

Finally, add a contrasting orange paint to the background. After the paint has dried, you can use your black marker to create a black outline of the dancer over the top of your pencil marks.

Timeline

1834: Degas is born in Paris, France, to Auguste de Gas, a wealthy banker, and Celestine Musson.

1854: He starts to study painting.

1862: Degas meets Édouard Manet and other painters who will later be called Impressionists.

1872: He goes to New Orleans to stay with relatives of his mother.

1874: His father dies, leaving large debts. At the same time, Degas helps organize the first Impressionist exhibition in Paris.

1886: Degas stops showing his work in public.

1908: Degas's eyesight becomes very poor. He starts to makes sculptures.

1917: Degas dies in Paris.

Glossary

canvas: Strong, uncolored cloth, used as a surface for oil painting.

composition: The arrangement of objects and people in a picture.

contrast: To be very different from something else.

Impressionist: One of a group of artists who tried to show objects as they appeared at a single glance.

pastel: A soft, colored, chalklike crayon used for drawing.

portrait: A painting that is intended to show a recognizable person.

pose: A position that someone stands in to be drawn or painted.

print: An image that is intended to be copied many times.

sketch: A rough drawing that is often done in preparation for making a larger painting.

studio: A room where an artist works.

traditional: Something that has been done in the same way for a long time.

Further information

BOOKS

Greenwood, Katie. *Degas: Great Lives in Graphic Form*. Ammonite Press, 2017.

Venezia, Mike. *Edgar Degas: Getting to Know the World's Greatest Artists*. Children's Press, 2016.

Wood, Alix. *Edgar Degas: Great Artists of the World*. Franklin Watts, 2015.

MUSEUMS

You can see Edgar's famous paintings from this book in these museums:

The Bellelli Family
Musée d'Orsay, Paris, France

The Cotton Exchange, New Orleans
Musée des Beaux-Arts de Pau, France

Racehorses at Longchamp
Museum of Fine Art, Boston, Massachusetts, United States

The Rehearsal
The Burrell Collection, Glasgow, Scotland

Miss La La at the Cirque Fernando
The National Gallery, London, England

Women Ironing
Musée d'Orsay, Paris, France

Combing the Hair
The National Gallery, London, England

WEBSITES

www.theartgallery.com.au/ArtEducation/greatartists/Degas/about/
Check out this introduction to Edgar with a timeline.

www.degas-painting.info/degasstyle.htm
Learn about Edgar's style and techniques.

www.edgar-degas.org/
Read information about Edgar's life and his paintings.

Index